THE BOYHOOD OF CHRIST

EXALTING THE MOTHER AND HER SON

See page 42.

THE

BOYHOOD

OF

CHRIST

BY

LEW WALLACE
Author of "Ben Hur" and "The Fair God"

ILLUSTRATED

Fredonia Books
Amsterdam, The Netherlands

The Boyhood of Christ

by
Lew Wallace

ISBN 1-58963-163-3

Copyright © 2001 by Fredonia Books

Reprinted from the 1893 edition

Fredonia Books
Amsterdam, The Netherlands
http://www.fredoniabooks.com

In order to make original editions of historical works available to scholars at an economical price, this facsimile of the original edition of 1893 is reproduced from the best available copy and has been digitally enhanced to improve legibility, but the text remains unaltered to retain historical authenticity.

PREFACE.

SHOULD one ask of another, or wonder to himself, why I, who am neither minister of the Gospel, nor theologian, nor churchman, have presumed to write this book, it pleases me to answer him respectfully—I wrote it to fix an impression distinctly in my mind.

Asks he for the impression thus sought to be fixed in my mind, then I would be twice happy did he content himself with this other answer— the Jesus Christ in whom I believe was, in all the stages of his life, a human being. His divinity was the Spirit within him, and the Spirit was God.

L. W.

CRAWFORDSVILLE, IND.,
June. 1888.

ILLUSTRATIONS.

The time draws near the birth of Christ;
The moon is hid; the night is still;
The Christmas bells from hill to hill
Answer each other in the mist."

THE BOYHOOD OF CHRIST.

"LET us go see Uncle Midas."

"Oh yes! Let us go and have him talk to us."

Outside the house all was winter, still and cold; inside were summer warmth, a rosy glow of light, and music and merry voices; for it was Christmas eve, and the young people of the town had met to celebrate it. Uncle Midas held that such was the right welcome of the glad event. The sweetest song men ever heard was that of the singers who came with the Annunciator; and arguing that the lesson was cheerfulness and joy, the old gentleman opened his doors to the boys and girls, and was himself happy, knowing they were happy.

2

Now, she who at the moment thought of Uncle Midas, and said let us go see him, and she who answered so willingly, were more than girls, yet not quite young women. They carried their childish names, but had lovers, each a number of them; and while they would laugh and dance and never tire, 'midst it all they could allow a serious thought. The first of the two to speak was Nan, the other was Puss, and in their dissimilarity they were pretty. Moreover, for persons so young they were well read, and could talk of great events and take delight in hearing of far countries. So, leaving the waltzes and the fiddling and merriment, and the harmless play that leads to love, and the dear delusions so like love that even the wise often yield to their enchantment only to find themselves mistaken, the two, hand in hand, stole out of the parlor door on the way to Uncle Midas.

They came first to a conservatory full of verdant treasures. Amongst them, specially in favor, were a palm-tree bearing stoneless dates, and a vine loaded with black grapes large as damson-plums. "This," Uncle Midas would say of the palm, "was given me by the monks of Mar-Saaba. The tree I saw them cut it from was the only green thing in their grim monastery. And this" — the vine — "was from a garden just outside the walls of Jerusalem. Of such were the grapes of Eshcol. And see there," he would say of a certain dwarfish shrub; "I plucked an acorn from the oak at Mamre, where the angels rested with the patriarch. Two thousand years hence it might be suggestive of its paternity." There were but few flowers under the glass roof. "Flowers remind me of nothing so much as their frailty, but these"—and he would look proudly and kindly at the palm and the out-stretching vine and their less ambitious accessories—"these keep me reminded of famous places I have seen, of persons, and of the ventures with which my days of nerve and will were seasoned. When at last one comes to live in the by-gone, as I am living, it is good to have such dependents always at his door to salute him, 'Hey, you remember this?' or 'Have you forgotten that?' Yon pomegranate, for example. I wrenched it from the terrace of a Greek garden on the Bosporus, and now if I stop to lighten it of a dead twig, it begins straightway whispering to me of misty mornings breaking over great ships coming and going in endless processions, and of afternoon dreams dreamed in caïques drifting along the empurpled shores of the hill-bound bay of Buyukdere."

Passing through the conservatory, the visitors, by a door overhung with sheeny *portières*, entered a study which was itself a study. With respect to interiors, proportions are always perfect when they raise no questions. No one ever asked Uncle Midas about the height of this room, or its length and breadth. There was in the centre a carpet from the looms of Smyrna, deep-tufted, and of indigo blue almost black. A desk of rose-tinted cherry-wood in the middle of the carpet was overlooked by a " Pensieroso " of Angelo in Castellina marble. As there was but one door, so there was but one window, and it, too, was richly draped. Bookcases of cherry, much carven, hung from three sides. A flame burned brightly in a broad open fireplace, and an old gold-colored rug of Khorassan caught the light of the flame, and held it in lustrous imprisonment. A circular window

THE SHEPHERDS GOING TO THE WORSHIP

in the shallow arch of the ceiling permitted day in its hours to flood the interior, until the lettering of the books. on shelves not higher than an easy hand-reach, sparkled like jewelry.

It is hardly enough to call the chamber a study. Uncle Midas had led a busy life; he had been a lawyer, a soldier, an author, and a traveller; he had dabbled in art, diplomacy, and politics; and, like most men so diversely occupied, there had never been a day in which he had not promised himself to let his mind say to his body, "Thou hast served me well, and carried me about for much teaching, and I have profited much; now, O good servant, take thine ease; the gathered fruits are waiting, and I alone will continue to labor." At length, noting the coming of his mid-afternoon of life, he determined to make the promise good. Towards that end he built the study, and tied it to his house with the conservatory, reserving the shelves for those other and higher associates which, in their cloaks of cloth and gold, would also wait for him, and, being called, begin talking in a manner the cleverest tongue cannot attain, and of every possible theme of human interest. For such are books! With good women, they are the superlative solace of waning years. Then, the preparations all complete, he retired from the pursuits which have their origin in ambition, and betook himself to study and reflection, believing that the capacity to think was a necessary accomplishment for the next life, and that it could be carried there with him. The sick and desponding sometimes take to their chairs, grimly waiting for death; but in perfect health, with a plentiful reserve of strength, a contentment which with him was but another name for charity, and a satisfaction perpetually exercising itself in finding excuses for the follies and frailties of strangers as well as acquaintances, he sat down in his study calmly and with deliberate forethought, that his soul might educate and fit itself for the life to come. "And this," he used to say, "shall no man be able to do except he believe in Jesus Christ."

Now, when the visitors had come into the study, they saw Uncle Midas in his rocking-chair before the fire, and as they ran to him they cried out, cheerily, "Oh, Uncle Midas!"

And he arose and answered as cheerily, "Heigh! Puss—and Nan!"

And he would have got them chairs, for he was a gentleman faithful to all the canons of the old school; but they divined his purpose, and were quicker than he; and when the chairs were brought and set at his right near his arm, and he was seated, they kissed him affectionately.

Uncle Midas, it must be said, did not look his sixty and five years. He was tall, white-haired, and white-mustached. This evening he was in slippers and dressing-gown. A gray silk cap had the effect to deepen the ineradicable sun-tan of his cheeks.

"Well, well," he said, "yonder are beaux and music and dance; here there is only an old man; yet you leave them and come to him?"

"Yes; we have come to hear you talk," said Nan.

A wave of music, splashing through the open door, streamed into the study.

"Hark!" he said. "Who may talk to young people against fiddles timing a waltz?"

"You can—and must," said Puss.

"Must?" he repeated.

"That was the word;" and the pretty girl, resting her elbows on the arm of his chair, looked up under his brows with an infinite persuasion in her blue eyes. His hand dropped upon her shoulder.

"I see I must; but—did you think to bring a subject with you?"

"Yes, indeed."

"You were very wise."

"It was—" She glanced appealingly at Nan; and Nan answered with a bright look, "The Boyhood of Christ."

Uncle Midas turned his face to the fire; then his head dropped lower, allowing the flame to redden his forehead and repeat itself in his eyes. The suggestion was plainly a surprise to him.

"Why that subject?" he asked, to gain a little time.

"Because it's Christmas eve."

"Yes, yes; I had almost forgotten."

"And then," Puss added, "it is so hard to think of him as a boy—I mean to think of him running, jumping, playing marbles, flying kites, spinning tops, and going about all day on mis-

THE SHEPHERDS AT THE CAVE

chiefs, such as throwing stones and robbing birds'-nests."

Uncle Midas looked up with a grave smile.

"Rest you, little friend," he said; "if the Nazarene lads of his day had tops, marbles, and kites —I am not sure they had—I would prefer to believe he found enjoyment in them."

"Oh, Uncle Midas!"

The good man's smile vanished.

"I see," he said, "you are going the way of the many; by-and-by you will not be able to think of our Lord as a man. To me his human birth was as much a divine fact as anything in all his sublime story."

Uncle Midas turned to the fire again, as if to assure himself of an idea.

"I find my love of God," he presently resumed, "does not of itself help me stand up under the unutterable thought of Him. He is so beyond my comprehension. But for Christ—ah, how different my feeling! He is my friend, my brother; I could have borne to look into his face; I could have even laid my head fearlessly upon his breast. Why? Because he was a man—a man capable

3

of returning my love in vastest measure, and therefore of easy understanding — a man who actually died for me, and of whose dying I am so much better."

At this he stopped; whereupon the fiddles, taking advantage of the silence, flung some of their liveliest notes into the study.

"Did you ever hear any one deny the human nature of the Saviour? I never did," said Nan, solemnly.

"But there are plenty to skip it as unbecoming their ideal of him," Uncle Midas replied, sharply. And then continued: "Two pictures always present themselves when I think of our Lord in his character of Man. A little plain near Bethlehem is illuminated in the night-time by a light dropped from the sky; and in the light there is movement and the flashing of wings, and one figure of indescribable majesty speaks to some cowering shepherds, 'Glory to God in the highest, and on earth peace, good-will to men.' This was the second annunciation, and the beautiful speech is a simple definition of the relation of Christ to men. And then the scene changes, giving me to see three crosses planted upon a low hill with millions of people around it; and there is a gloom, almost darkness, in which the crosses rock to and fro, yielding to an earthquake, and upon one of them a man, nailed hands and feet, lifts his face, over-hung with bloody locks, and cries, as if expiring, 'Father, into Thy hands I commend my spirit.' And the awfulness of the sight, my little friends, does not hide from me that the sufferer, dying as he was, tarried a moment to make definition of his relation to God."

Uncle Midas's voice shook; he was evidently very much in earnest; and while he rested, possibly to give his fair listeners time to comprehend his argument, there was a quick step behind the party, and they all turned to a new-comer. Again Uncle Midas would have risen, but Puss stayed him.

"It's only John," she said.

The person so familiarly spoken of approached.

"Do not move," he said to Uncle Midas. " I come to tell Puss that the quadrille is forming, and if she wants to be in it, we must hurry."

Uncle Midas glanced at John and Puss, and

smiled. "It's only John," meant a great deal to him.

"Thank you," she replied; "I will not dance now. Uncle is talking. Bring a chair and join us. He will not object, I am sure."

Then, when John was seated, Uncle Midas said, "As the young man has kindly consented to be of our audience, it is but fair, Puss, that you tell him of what we are talking." And Puss did so, after which Uncle Midas proceeded: "The vision of the Crucifixion never visits me without another—a veritable picture hanging in the Pitti Gallery in Florence—the 'Ecce Homo' of Carlo Dolce. In artistic phrase, it is an idealization of the face of Christ, yet there is much more of it than a mere face. An ordinary expert can make features in likeness, but the rendition on canvas of a thought, a passion, an emotion of the soul, a face being used for the purpose, is a subtlety of genius of the highest order; and then the picture is in fact a portrait of the thought, passion, or emotion. In this sense the 'Ecce Homo' of which I am speaking is a portrait of the agony of Christ dying, and to me

THE MOTHER IN EGYPT REPOSING.

there is nothing in the world of art of such overpowering effect. The crown of thorns, the dusty, clotted locks, the blood-drops and sweat-stains, are utilized; but they do no more than identify the subject and the moment. There is no contraction of brow or writhing of facial muscle; the lower lip hangs a little apart, a deadly pallor overcasts the countenance, the eyes—ah, therein lies the achievement! Even in their faintness they somehow fasten upon the beholder, and say to him, with a pathos far beyond the power of words, 'See to what I have been brought — I who came to tell you of a loving God, of resurrection after death, of a better life in store for you—I who only asked you to love and believe in me!'"

"I will certainly see that picture when I get to Florence," said John, who had been listening with the sharpest intensity.

Uncle Midas waved his hand gently. "And you will then understand the lesson it taught me. As the artist could not have painted the agony of the Lord without giving us his face, so it is not possible for us to be convinced of his divinity except by the self-comparisons which a recognition of his human nature affords."

"But, Uncle—" said Nan.

"I hear you," he answered, with a glance which as much as said he knew her thought.

"You were to talk to us about—"

She hesitated.

"About the boyhood," he said, smiling. "Well, little one, your reminder only satisfies me that my preface has not failed its object. You are impatient to hear the kind of boy such a man as Christ was; and we will now inquire if he had a boyhood, except as the years of that stage of life can be so called."

The old gentleman drew his brows down over his eyes, gazed into the fire a while, looked up again, and asked, "Perhaps, Nan, you can tell me the incidents in which the Lord as a child is made to appear in the Scriptures?"

"Yes: when the shepherds came to worship him; at the visit of the Magi; the flight into Egypt; the presentation in the Temple; and when he was found with the doctors at the end of the Passover."

"Thank you, dear," Uncle Midas said, with a bow; then immediately continued: "Now is it not amazing that the youth of one who intended so well and actually did so much, who left us the most pathetic of histories, who will remain forever the perfect standard of comparative holiness, applicable alike to every phase and circumstance of human life, whose hold upon men has already proven him a prophet unto himself, and still goes on widening and deepening—how wonderful, I say, that the childhood of such a man should be so beggarly of authentic incident!"

"But is it so?" asked John, impulsively. "I am sure I have somewhere heard anecdotes of his infancy, if not his boyhood."

"Very likely," said Uncle Midas: "and a word or two of them. The people who had actually seen the Saviour were hardly passed away before the incompleteness of the records pertaining to him became painfully manifest, especially to the controversialists who had zealously espoused his teachings. The authors of the four canonical Gospels were not biographers in the modern sense of the word. In their great anxiety to get large facts set down imperishably they overlooked the small. For example, so the Sermon on the Mount were reported, of what importance was it to them to tell of the Master's appearance? and whether he had blue eyes or black, or was fair or dark, or tall or short, or lean or fat? The incidents of his birth are copious, yet as we read.them there comes to us a feeling that they would have been cut shorter had it not been essential to establish his coming into the world in exact fulfilment of the prophecies. There is no mistaking the nationality of the four apostolic *clerks.* Relatively to the year 36, which was that of the Crucifixion, there is a non-agreement as to the times in which they wrote. One learned man says St. Matthew's book was completed two years after the sad event; St. Luke's, fifteen years after; St. Mark's, twenty-seven; and St. John's, thirty-three. Yet later, when the hunger of piety seized the world, numbers of men of sanctity betook themselves to the duty, as they conceived it, of supplying missing data. The second, third, and fourth centuries were prolific in such works. Saintly recluses enlivened the loneliness of their cells and caverns

THEN THEY PURSUED ON FROM CITY TO CITY, CASTING OUT SATANS AS THEY WENT, AND HEALING LEPERS, AND THE SICK AND MISERABLE.' "

by writing and rewriting, each in a style mod-
elled more or less after the Scriptures, the legends
of the Holy Family with which the Christian East
abounded. Very often they resorted to downright
invention, coloring the product with their pious
inclinations. Seventy such screeds, all now lost,
are known from mention in living books, and
they must have been but a few of the many.
Enough have survived to give us an idea of the
assortment. The tale of Christ's descent into hell
belongs to the class—a bold conception that may
have had to do with Milton's great epic. We
hear also of a hymn our Lord is said to have
taught his disciples, and the thought of it is sufficient to beget a wish that the lines had been
preserved ; the novelty of the fancy attracts us
that much at least. Under the sanction of time
the vagaries of which I am speaking entered into
the faith of Christians to an astonishing degree.
In the monkish era of England they served the
clergy as foundations for the holiday spectacles
with which they so successfully impressed the
illiterate peasantry. Still later, in the fifteenth
century, as great a personage as Francis I. had

4

them dressed up as a drama, entitled 'The Grand
Mystery of the Acts of the Apostles.' The perform-
ance, crowded, it is said, with four hundred and
eighty-five *dramatis personæ*, was given in Paris,
and filled several days, reminding us of the Passion Play of the Shi-ite Mohammedans, still of
annual repetition in India, requiring when fully
rendered eleven days. The affecting tragedy
displayed at Oberammergau is not an original
conception. Coming to my purpose, however"
—and Uncle Midas filled a pause with a pleasant look darted at the circle, as if to pray pardon,
and give assurance that he had had a point all
the time in view—"the stories my young friend
alludes to are mostly to be found in a book called
'The First Gospel of the Infancy of Jesus Christ.'
There is another of the same school, but purely
reiterative, and so inferior as to be unworthy no-
tice. The so-called 'First Gospel,' if its origin is
correctly stated, is referable to the second century at least, as in that period there was a sect
known as Gnostics who received it implicitly.
We are also told of a number of deeply learned
and illustrious Fathers of the Church who flour-

ished in succeeding times, and read and believed it, amongst others Athanasius and Chrysostom. It has even been charged that Mahomet drew from its pages while he was composing portions of the Koran. The most curious circumstance connected with it, however, is the Persian legend —that our Lord was a dyer by trade, and once wrought a miracle with colors; and such credit is said to have been given the myth that the Persian dyers held him in reverence as their patron, and actually styled their dye - houses *Shops of Christ.*"

"Shocking!" exclaimed Puss.

"And to call that reverence! Fie on you, Uncle!" added Nan.

The old gentleman smiled submissively as he replied: "The description seemed to require the word. And then we should not forget that while as a sentiment reverence may be universally the same it nevertheless admits of the widest differences in expression. The dyers thought they were doing our Lord the highest honor. But let me on. This 'First Gospel of the Infancy' was past venture the hive into which the legends devised to meet the want of knowledge of Christ in the morning of his earthly life were drawn together. The author—or authors, if you please —had it in heart to exalt the mother and her son. The one he calls the Lady St. Mary, the other the Lord Jesus. The quality of the epithets he uses are above criticism; more than respectful, they are endearing. Happily the accessaries that go with the incidents of his narrative at once expose him as a believer without judgment, a man determined to fill at least one void in the Chronicles, if he can, regardless of truth, and uncontrolled by the slightest sense of fitness or consistency."

"Do you remember any of the stories?" asked a listener.

"Oh yes."

"Some of us have never heard them."

A look as if something unpleasant had been suggested to him deepened the wrinkle between Uncle Midas's brows; but it was momentary.

"I do not like them, my young friends," he answered, somewhat slowly. "They detract from the exceeding holiness of the personages of whom

BUT WHEN I SAW THIS WOMAN, AND THIS
LITTLE INFANT WITH HER.'"

they are told, and are utterly out of character. At the same time it must be admitted that I have gone too far in speaking of them to now dismiss them summarily. You are entitled to examples sufficient to show you how trifling and puerile they are."

The auditors, as at a signal, drew closer about the old gentleman's chair, and when all was quiet he continued:

"The writer begins with the birth, but tells nothing about it of importance not better told by good old St. Matthew. He gives himself free rein, however, when describing the wanderings of the Holy Family in Egypt. In that episode, so interesting to the imagination of every Gospel reader, he makes the Lady St. Mary the principal character. As if she were a vulgar show-woman of the miraculous powers of her son, and they a subject of common pride, she exhibits them in the towns along the way, and in compensation accepts entertainments and presents. Sometimes she takes to the road quite enriched. Through the child, it is true, she in instances brings good to unhappy people; yet, with a

strange unmindfulness on the author's part of
the necessity that drove Joseph out of Judea,
the results are of a kind to excite report vast
enough to reach the remorseless King still alive
and watchful up in the palace on Mount Zion.

"With a vanity of faith almost pardonable,
the story-teller thought it of first importance to
signalize the advent of the precious fugitives
into the new south-country. With that intent
he informs us they came to a great city. Passing its name and locality, he gravely assures us
that the journey thither was so long that the
girths of the Lady St. Mary's saddle broke. The
city was the home of an idol to which all the
other idols and gods of Egypt brought offerings
and vows. As if that were not enough to give
us a just idea of how very great this particular
idol was, we are further told that it was an
intimate of Satan's, and that through its chief
priest it was in the habit of taking the Egyp-
tians into confidence, and telling them all the
arch-enemy told it. Joseph and Mary betook
themselves to an inn which happened to be
close to the temple of the master idol, and their

mere presence there astonished the city and
filled the land with fear. Presently the magis-
trates and priests ran together, asking what
was the matter, and the idol answered, 'The
Unknown God is come hither, beside whom no
other is entitled to worship. He it is that
makes all the trembling of men and lesser dei-
ties.' Thereupon, as if to confirm the news, the
distinguished idol fell down, and the noise of
his fall was so prodigious that all Egypt and
the peoples of the countries near by assembled,
presumably to take counsel what they should
do. In such phrase the simple story-teller, for-
getful of Herod and the myrmidons whom that
monster had out scouring everywhere, exalts our
Lord. And so it has always been, when writ-
ers would mount into the ultimate sublime, they
set the gods to fighting and wear themselves
out giving us to see the battle."

"Well, Uncle, in this instance the victory was
given where it belongs," said Puss, demurely.

"True enough," Uncle Midas replied, with an
approving smile; "but the tale does not stop
there. The devout old romancer must needs in-

crease the glory won. He accordingly holds the curtain aside while the Lady St. Mary proceeds to perform her first direct miracle. It appears that the priest of the demolished idol had a son three years old 'possessed with a multitude of devils of many strange utterances,' who moved the poor child to tear his clothes and throw stones at passers-by."

"How old was he?"

"The chronicle says three years—certainly an uncommon example of precocious wickedness. About the time that everybody, except the three travellers, were up at the temple, the unfortunate came to the inn flushed with all his tormentors. What grief might have befallen, and to whom, we are not left to conjecture, for the Lady St. Mary had a little before washed the swaddling clothes of the Lord Christ, and hung them upon a post to dry. The visitor took one of them and put it upon his head, whereupon a cloud of devils poured out of his mouth, and as crows and serpents flew away."

There was a disposition to laugh at this *dé-noûment,* but Uncle Midas checked it with a

TO DECK HIMSELF FROM THE ANEMONE-BEDS
OF THE HILLS.'"

negative shake of the hand, and was about to
go on when a lad ran in and called out, "H'lo!
Partners for the dance! The fiddlers are waiting." But seeing the group around the chair,
he joined it, and forgot his errand. Then Uncle
Midas, well pleased, continued:

"The next adventure was with robbers. Joseph and the Lady St. Mary, when they heard
that the idol was destroyed, were afraid, and cast
about, counselling what they should do. Taking
a bold resolution, they left the inn hastily, and
fled to a place notoriously the haunt of outlaws,
who made it a practice to rob travellers and
carry them away. The story-teller does not say
so, but it is likely that the 'knights of the road'
of that day set the custom of holding their prisoners for ransom yet observed by brigands of the
East, and, like the latter, they may have gone
the length of cutting ears off for the first failure
to pay, and noses for the second. Presumably
Joseph's goods were neither many nor of great
value; but the life of the young child was
worth the world many times over - appraised.
Hardly was he come to the perilous place when

5

the thieves heard what is fittingly described ' as
the noise of a king with a great army, and many
horse, and the trumpets sounding.' Then thinking, doubtless, that justice was upon them, they
in turn were panic-struck, and ran, leaving all
their plunder ; whereat the prisoners set themselves free, and took each his own goods, and
as they were going they met Joseph and the
Lady St. Mary. 'Where is that king who scared
the robbers off ?' they asked ; and Joseph, as
became a diplomat, replied, ' He will come after
us.' "

At this conclusion the young people clapped
their hands, and pressed Uncle Midas to proceed,
and he did so :

" The Holy Family at length arrived at another
city, and seeing there a woman possessed with
a devil the Lady St. Mary pitied her ; and the
merciful thought of the pure sweet heart was
of itself enough, for immediately, in the quaint
language of the chronicler, ' Satan left her, and
fled away in the form of a young man, saying,
" Wo to me, because of thee, Mary, and thy
Son." ' "

This time the mirth of the girls was much excited, so that it was difficult to suppress it.

"Let us not laugh," Uncle Midas said. "The writer was serious. He intended as best he could to honor our Lord. The stories may be absurd, yet the faith they show is beautiful. Our next is dashed with poetry. The morning after the miracle, for which, as we have seen, the simple pity of the Lady St. Mary was so effective, the Holy Family took the road again. Any of the pictures of the old masters classified as *reposes* will tell us how they journeyed — the Lady St. Mary on a donkey, with the child in her lap, while Joseph, cane in hand, toiled solemnly on afoot, punching the beast now and then lest it should go to sleep and stumble. In the evening they came to another town, where they found a strange state of affairs. The people were going about with every sign of sorrowful excitement. A company had met at a house to celebrate a marriage; but, alas! And Satan came also, and with him a band of sorcerers, who so wrought that in the part of the ceremony where the bride is required to say something—possibly 'Yes'—she could not. She was struck dumb. The chronicler says she could not even open her mouth."

As this point offered a chance for witticisms on the side of the young men of Uncle Midas's party, they cast looks at each other without interrupting the story.

"The poor dumb bride," Uncle Midas continued, " chanced to be where she could see the Lady St. Mary riding into the town, with the dear Lord Christ in her lap. She ran with out-stretched hands and caught the baby to her breast, and fondled and caressed it as only women can, but not mutely, as you would suppose; for on the instant the tie of her tongue was broken, and she sang praises unto him who had restored her. And there was joy to the bridegroom, joy to the family, joy to all the town that night. The entertainment of the travellers was so generous and splendid that they abode there several days.

"Then they pursued on from city to city, casting out Satans as they went, and healing lepers, and the sick and miserable, and always doing good. All very pleasant, except that at times, as if it were not possible to conceal the earthiness of his ideas, the author permits Joseph to go away handsomely rewarded with gifts."

"But they had to live," suggested one of the young men.

"Yes, that is the practical view," said Uncle Midas, with slight impatience. "But if you will excuse me, another of the stories comes to mind that should be given, since it shows the old writer at his best. Indeed, for characterization and dramatic movement it would serve our *raconteurs* of short tales as a model of their art. To do the old writer justice, you shall have it in his own words."

Thereupon the old gentleman arose, and going to a shelf, took out a book and returned with it.

"Turn on the light there," he ordered from his seat; and when that was done to his satisfaction, "I will read now," he said; "only observe how much the style and language resemble the matchless simplicity of the 'Pilgrim's Progress.'" And then he began:

"'But going forward on the morrow, they came

to another city, and saw three women going from a certain grave with great weeping. When St. Mary saw them she spake to the girl who was their companion, saying, "Go and inquire of them what is the matter with them, and what misfortune has befallen them." When the girl asked them they made her no answer, but asked her again, "Who are ye? and where are ye going? For the day is far spent, and night is at hand." "We are travellers," saith the girl, "and are seeking for an inn to lodge at." They replied, "Go along with us, and lodge with us." They then followed them, and were introduced into a new house, well furnished with all sorts of new furniture.

"'It was now winter-time, and the girl went into the parlor where these women were, and found them weeping and lamenting as before. By them stood a mule, which they kissed and were feeding; it was covered over with silk, and had an ebony collar hanging down from its neck. But when the girl said, "How handsome, ladies, that mule is!" they replied with tears, and said, "This mule which you see was our brother—"'"

THEY WATCHED HIM WITH JEALOUS CARE

"Oh!" cried Nan.

" ' " — our brother, born of the same mother as we. For when our father died, and left us a very large estate, and we had only this brother, and we endeavored to procure him a suitable match, and thought he should be married as other men, some giddy and jealous women bewitched him without our knowledge; and we one night, a little before day, while the doors of the house were all fast shut, saw this our brother was changed into a mule, such as you now see him to be; and we, in the melancholy condition in which you see us, having no father to comfort us, have applied to all the wise men, magicians, and diviners in the world, but they have been of no service to us. As often, therefore, as we find ourselves oppressed with grief, we rise and go with this our brother to our father's tomb, where, when we have cried sufficiently, we return home."

" ' When the girl had heard this, she said, "Take courage, and cease your fears, for you have a remedy for your afflictions near at hand, even among you, and in the midst of your house; for

I was also leprous; but when I saw this woman, and this little infant with her, whose name is Jesus, I sprinkled my body with the water with which his mother had washed him, and I was presently made well. And I am certain that he is also capable of relieving you under your distress. Wherefore arise, go to my mistress Mary, and when you have brought her into your parlor, disclose to her the secret, at the same time earnestly beseeching her to compassionate your case."

" 'As soon as the women had heard the girl's discourse they hastened away to the Lady St. Mary, introduced themselves to her, and sitting down before her, they wept, and said, " O our Lady St. Mary, pity your handmaids, for we have no head of our family, no one older than us; no father or brother to go in and out before us; but this mule which you see was our brother, which some women by witchcraft have brought into this condition which you see. We therefore entreat you to compassionate us."

" ' Hereupon St. Mary was grieved at their case, and taking the Lord Jesus, put him upon the back of the mule, and said to her son, "O Jesus Christ, restore according to thy extraordinary power this mule, and grant him to have again the shape of a man and a rational creature, as he had formerly." This was scarce said by the Lady St. Mary but the mule immediately passed into a human form, and became a young man without any deformity. Then he and his mother and the sisters worshipped the Lady St. Mary, and lifting the child upon their heads, they kissed him, and said, "Blessed is thy mother, O Jesus, O Saviour of the world! Blessed are the eyes which are so happy as to see thee!" Then both the sisters told their mother, saying, "Of a truth our brother is restored to his former shape by the help of the Lord Jesus Christ and the kindness of that girl who told us of Mary and her son."'"

Here Uncle Midas, who had been acquitting himself as a reader very handsomely indeed, drew the lids of the book together, though marking the place with the first finger between the pages, and asked, with a sly look, "That sounds like the end, don't it?"

"Stories nowadays end with weddings," some one suggested.

"And so they did in the beginning. So does this one. There were critics abroad the day it was written, seventeen hundred years ago, and a public to please, and doubtless the author stood in awe of them as authors now do, else the following is a base interpolation. Listen!—

"'And inasmuch as our brother is unmarried, it is fit that we marry him to this girl, their servant. When they had consulted St. Mary in the matter, and she had given her consent, they made a splendid wedding for the girl.'"

There was clapping of hands at that, and laughter; and the interruption did not in the least disconcert Uncle Midas, who calmly proceeded with his reading.

"'And so their sorrow being turned into gladness, and their mourning into mirth, they began to rejoice, and make merry, and sing, being dressed in their richest attire, with bracelets.... After this Joseph and Mary tarried there ten days, then went away, having received great re-

MARY TEACHING JESUS THE ALPHABET

spect from those people, who, when they took their leave of them and returned home, cried, but especially the girl.' "

Then, when the humor of his party was spent, Uncle Midas said, "I fear I am keeping you too long. The fiddlers are waiting."

"No, no! Go on!" the party answered, unanimously.

"Very well, we will at least dispose of the old story - teller, and shortly; for in truth his tales soon begin to show a failure of ingenuity, and he suffers them to drop into a dismal monotony of circumstance. That of Titus and Dumachus is the only one succeeding those I have given that is marked with the slightest cunning. The Holy Family is again led by Joseph amongst thieves, but this time they are all asleep. At the last moment two of them wake up; an altercation ensues between them. One proves to be kindly disposed, and he insists that Joseph be allowed to pass. Titus is his name, and he finally prevails, but not until he has given the other, Dumachus, his girdle. Then the Lord is made to come distinctly forward as a prophet. He tells the Lady St. Mary that in thirty years he will be crucified, with Titus on his right hand and Dumachus on his left, and that the former shall go before him into Paradise.

"After this second escape from highwaymen the travellers go on to a city of several idols, which are appropriately turned into hills of sand.

"They then come to Matarea, a place of but little importance at that time, since it is described as a sycamore-tree—the same, probably, that is made to appear in so many *reposes.* From Matarea the wanderers at last reach Memphis, where they see Pharaoh, and abide three years, performing many miracles. At the close of that period they return to Judea; with which, as the old chronicler sees them, the Infancy closes and the Boyhood begins.

"Thereupon a new line of incidents is disclosed to us. The Lady St. Mary disappears as a show-woman. Our Lord himself becomes chief actor, and the performances are nearly all located in and about Nazareth. A close study of the book from this point leads to a suspicion that a new hand has been put to the work.

Our Saviour is presented to us not merely as a boy, but—if the apparent irreverence of the remark can be excused—as a very bad boy. The Divine Power still attends him, and he trifles with it. He gets angry with his playmates, and does them serious mischief, insomuch that their parents complain of him. He terrorizes the town. At seven years of age he is reputed a sorcerer. One day, with other lads, he was making birds and animals of clay, and to excel them he said boastfully that his figures should walk and fly, and they did all he ordered them. Of like kind, only more malicious, was his dealing with the dyer. Finding parcels of cloth in the poor man's shop, left to be variously colored, he threw them all into one kettle. The shopkeeper set up a great cry. To appease him our Lord asked what colors they were to have been, and being told, he took the pieces out each of the desired color. There is little wonder that the dyers of Persia elected him their patron. Going, as it were, from bad to worse, another of the absurd tales is of his turning his playmates into kids. Malice unrelieved distinguishes the legend of his striking the son of Hanani dead for wasting the water he had collected into a miniature fish-pond. In yet another we are gravely told that, as he was returning home with Joseph, a boy ran against him so hard as to throw him down. Then our Lord, in great wrath, arose and cried out, 'Thou too shalt fall, and never rise.' That moment the boy fell down dead."

"That is awful!" exclaimed John.

"Worse than awful," Uncle Midas rejoined, warmly. "Now and then, however, the wickedness is varied by something solemnly ludicrous. Take, for example, the statement that Joseph was in the habit of carrying the Son of Mary along with him when he went about the country mending gates, milk-pails, sieves, and boxes; for having spoiled the job, as he was almost certain to do, the lad was needed to set it to rights. Or, in the quaintness of the original, 'as often as Joseph had anything in his work to make longer or shorter, or wider or narrower, the Lord Jesus would stretch his hand towards it, and presently it became as Joseph would have

it.' A story of such delicious simplicity is added,
in illustration, that it would be inexcusable to
omit the telling in the chronicler's own words.
Premising that Joseph 'was not very skilful at
his carpenter's trade,' he says:

"'On a certain time the King of Jerusalem
sent for him, and said, "I would have thee make
me a throne of the same dimensions with that
place in which I commonly sit." Joseph obeyed,
and forthwith began the work, and continued
two years in the King's palace before he finished
it. And when he came to fix it in its place, he
found it wanting two spans on each side of the
appointed measure; which, when the King saw,
he was very angry with Joseph. And Joseph,
afraid of the King's anger, went to bed without
his supper, taking not anything to eat. Then
the Lord Jesus asked him what he was afraid of.
Joseph replied, "Because I have lost my labor
in the work which I have been about these two
years." Jesus said to him, "Fear not, neither be
cast down; do thou lay hold on one side, and I
will the other, and we will bring it to its just
dimensions." And when Joseph had done as

the Lord Jesus said, and each of them had with
strength drawn his side, the throne obeyed and
was brought to the proper dimensions of the
place. Which miracle, when they who stood by
saw, they were astonished and praised God. The
throne was made of the same wood which was in
being in Solomon's time, namely, wood adorned
with various shapes and figures.' "

The reading finished, Uncle Midas closed the
volume, saying, emphatically, " Enough ! The
book has place on my shelf along with other
religious literary curiosities, such as the Koran
and the Mormon Bible. I do not read any of
them now. They are only useful as instruments
for the measurement of the capacity of faith.
They teach me what all men religiously disposed
can be made believe. And now I will go back
to the point from which you started me. Do
you remember it, any of you ?"

" Yes," said Nan ; "you were speaking of the
scarcity of reliable incidents of the Saviour's
childhood."

" Quite right, dear ; and I have only to **say**
further that, as an argument, the circumstance

MARY TEACHING JESUS THE ALPHABET

seems at first glance to justify the opinion commonly held by thinkers, that the youth of our Lord ran on in course very much like that of the generality of poor Jewish children."

"I can't believe that, uncle," said Puss, with a show of indignation.

The old gentleman looked at her benignantly.

"Nor can I," he said. "They say that Joseph, to whom as a child our Lord was subject, was a carpenter who plied only the humbler branches of the trade, and that Mary, his wife, spun the flax and wool for the family, and was a housewife. These are the circumstances chiefly relied upon to support the theory that the condition of the child was poverty. Now while I admit the circumstances, I deny the conclusion. That Joseph was a carpenter signifies nothing, as the law required every Israelite, rich or poor, to follow some occupation. Then was it not written of the exemplar of all the mothers in Israel, 'She looketh well to the ways of her household, and eateth not the bread of idleness?' And if we may give heed to accounts not purely Scriptural, Mary owned the house in Nazareth in which

7

the family dwelt; but conforming to the Scriptures, it is to be remembered that amongst the
gifts of the Magi there was gold. And I please
myself thinking that there was enough of it to
support the holy family while it was in Egypt,
and afterwards in Nazareth. In my view, then,
the child was not born to poverty. If any one
doubts the conclusion, let him ponder the awful
declaration in the Talmud: 'These four are ac-
counted as dead: the blind, the leper, the *poor*,
and the childless.' As to the social position of
the family, it is enough to remark that, besides
being a just man, Joseph was a lineal descend-
ant of David the King."

"They were neither rich nor poor, then," said
John.

"Only comfortable," Uncle Midas rejoined; then
proceeded: "Exactly the condition to allow our
Saviour a marginal time in which to taste something of natural boyish freedom; to have little
playmates, run races with the youngest of the
flocks, deck himself from the anemone - beds on
the hills, and watch the clouds form slowly about
the summit of old Hermon. It must be noted,

however, that this period was shorter with him than with our lads, for the terrible Talmudic rules fell upon him early, after which there was small chance to enjoy boyhood according to our ideas of its enjoyment. By overwhelming men, women, and children with duties, they put existence in iron jackets. To neglect the rules, or the least of them, was to invoke perdition. And besides—" Uncle Midas drew his gray cap well down, and meditated a moment. " I was about to say," he then continued, " that there was another cause to cut short the jocund marginal period of our Lord, which must not be overlooked—a cause peculiar to himself, and, in my judgment, more influential even than the Talmudic rules. His precocity was miraculous. At a time when other children are muling in their mothers' arms, the cells of his understanding began to enlarge and fill with knowledge. The process must have been like the gradual rise of water in the basin of a spring ; at all events, the knowledge was of a kind to make him preternaturally serious, and it was not derived from books or school-masters."

"You think the angels waited upon him?" interposed Nan.

The question was asked with such artlessness that Uncle Midas, who had been talking with self-concentration, looked at her half startled.

"I did not think of being called upon to make the admission, my little friend," he said; "but I will—only do not take me to be a modern spiritualist. You may have seen copies of the most beautiful of the Virgin Mothers. Murillo did but work according to his faith when he filled the space about the central figure with faces of attending spirits. At the feet of the Sistine Madonna, beyond peradventure the most divinely perfect Mother and Child in group, there are two little cherubs inimitably suggestive of mischievous urchins; but examine them closely next time, and see what knowledge is conveyed in the expression of their countenances. Raphael painted them *con amore,* meaning that he believed in them—and so do I. I do not think such ministers go with us common mortals. Goodness help them if they do! That they went with the divine Child, however, I am quick to believe. They

LISTENING FOR VOICES

watched him with jealous care; they floated on
the clouds above him; they trod the air in his
chamber; they gave color, direction, purity, and
strength to his thought. His mother may have
taught him the alphabet, but neither she nor the
teachers in the synagogue could have helped him
to that other rarer and higher learning in the
light of which the hearts of those about him were
as primers for easy reading. Through what human agency was it that before he was a man he
was master of a lore which Hillel had not been
able to obtain with all his one hundred and
twenty years of studious life?"

Uncle Midas concluded this speech with something like declamation; unconsciously he had
become excited, and it was not a little to his
relief that other young people broke into the
study, and with whispers and smothered laughter
closed around the fire.

"Hush!" said John, severely. "Uncle Midas
is talking."

But Uncle Midas spoke more kindly: "I fear
the fiddlers will complain of me."

"Not just now," replied a girl as she rested

her arms on the back of his chair. "They are at the cold chicken and mulled cider on the sideboard."

"Never mind them, uncle," passed round in encouraging chorus.

As such was the general voice, he said: "Very well—only I am sorry the new-comers will have to guess what has preceded by the fragment that follows. My subject is the boyhood of Christ. I was saying I did not think he had much time to enjoy his, and will now add another argument in support of the opinion. Suppose by any chance he came while a child to know the mysteries of his birth. The effects would have been manifold, but of one of them I am certain — all desire for pastime by childish means would have then ended."

"Then you believe he knew it all?" asked Puss, impulsively—"knew it all when he was a child?"

"Well," he answered, "let us see. He was from the beginning in care of at least two persons who could not have put their knowledge of him away had they wished to do so. The world

has done injustice to Joseph. The fathers of the
Church did better when they canonized him.
He held a prodigious secret in his possession,
and was true to it. 'Who is this?' the rabbis
asked, when Christ began his miracles; and they
answered themselves, 'Oh, it is the carpenter's
son!' The other person was Mary, the mother.
After all that has been said and written of her
appearance, her devotion, her sanctity—her wom-
anliness makes her as incomparable amongst
women as her son is incomparable amongst men.
I am somewhat rigid in my idea that worship is
due to God alone; nevertheless, it would have
been hard for me to refuse to fall in and march
with Cyril in his great dispute with Nestorius,
and I am sensible of a kindly feeling for Pope
Gregory the Great, because he at length settled
the dispute by making it lawful to write 'Holy
Mother of God' after Mary's name. Neither have
I any disposition to quarrel with the devotional
habit the peasants have of stopping to kneel
before the Mother as she appears above the rural
altars on the way-sides of Italy. On the quay of
the Bosporus as one approaches Therapia there

is an arched vault of an ·ancient ruin in which
a poor hunch - backed Greek keeps a candle always burning before a wretched picture of the
Virgin. In front of that humble church I habit-
ually stopped my caïque, and going in, dropped
a piastre in the alms-box, and crossed myself.
The deformed keeper kept his light, such as it
was, burning in the world; my money helped
give him bread and maintain his light; the sign
was reverence to her who is to be the pattern of
mothers while the earth endures; and such worship as there was in my salutation and gift went
up to God with as much acceptance, in my be-
lief, as if it had been rendered with organ accom-
paniments amidst the splendors of St. Peter's."

There was a decided movement amongst the
audience at these words. Uncle Midas was allowing himself to be carried away again. The
rustle, however, brought him back to his subject.

"I beg your pardon," he said, with charming
candor. "If I have wandered a little, charge the
fault to my great love of good women. The two,
Joseph and Mary, I was saying, possessed the

THE BOY JESUS IN THE TEMPLE

secret of our Lord's origin. When I consider
their relationship to him, it becomes impossible
for me to think they did not tell him all they
knew about him. I prefer to believe the story
came first from her. She knew it best; she
loved him most; and as to the time the tale
was told, exactness is of no importance. The
hour, we may be sure, was auspicious; she held
him clasped in her arms; his head lay upon her
breast; from that soft pure pillow he looked up
into her eyes; and then she remembered that he
was the Messiah, and she the most blessed of
women, and from that moment he was lost to
all the claims of boyhood. In the good old language so nearly descriptive of the indescribable,
'The grace of God was upon him.'"

"Well, if he did not play as other children,
he at least went to school?" one of the auditors
said; and Uncle Midas hastened to reply:

"If Nazareth had a school — and the better
opinion is that the village was not so favored—
it is to be kept in mind that scholars could not
be admitted before the age of six, and that all
instruction was limited to the Law, and entirely

8

oral. The master sat on a raised seat; the children, on the floor, simply repeated what he recited to them until they knew the lesson by heart. After six years—certainly after he came to know himself—our Lord was taught, I think, by his mother. She may have initiated him in the alphabet earlier; anyhow I delight in imagining the two at work. The *torah* is spread upon her knee; he has a hand over her shoulder, she an arm about his waist; he is quick to apprehend; their voices are low and sweet; at times they turn to each other, and it is the old story—

'Soft eyes looked love to eyes that spake again.'"

Uncle Midas's voice was a little tremulous, but he went on in the same strain:

"After the lad came to know himself, the knowledge enforced solemnity and serious thought. The old master who painted him trudging after Joseph with a basket of tools had the true conception of him about this time, for he was humble and uncomplaining, and delighted in service. Of out-door employments, I am sure he most

loved that of the shepherd. In following the
capricious flocks, as they wandered over the
broad Esdraelon, he could freely indulge the ex-
pectancy of revelation that must have been his
constant condition of mind. I have had visions
of him out in the historic plain, sunburned, large-
eyed, oval-faced, leaning upon a crook, a dog by
his side. What time he is not observant of his
charge, he is listening for voices, attentive to
each passing wind, or gazing at the clouds for
seraphic messengers, or giving heed to the emo-
tions of his own being in the hope of their be-
coming telltales of all he so wished. How ten-
derly he would carry the weaklings of the herd
down the steeps and over the stony places! He
loved them, and they loved him. But—"

And Uncle Midas rested upon the word, and
thereupon the violins off in the parlor seemed
suddenly to find their liveliest notes. A peal
of Strauss's dance music penetrated the study,
though without effect; even the waltzers of the
party remained patiently around the old gentleman's chair. One little miss whispered, "We're
all here but the fiddlers."

"And they'll be along presently," another one replied.

"I was about to do what the lovers of our Lord have so often done," Uncle Midas at length said, confidently, as if he had overtaken the idea that was trying to escape him in the fire — "I was about to grumble again at the meagreness of the record; but let us do better—let us take up and eke out all we can of what there is. One of you get the Testament there on the table, and read from Luke ii., beginning with the 39th verse."

Presently the reading began.

"Observe," said Uncle Midas, after the 43d verse, "he is spoken of as the *child* Jesus. Jump now to 46 and 47."

The reader was attentive.

"'And it came to pass, that after three days they found him in the temple, sitting in the midst of the doctors, both hearing them, and asking them questions. And all that heard him were astonished at his understanding and answers.'"

"Rest there," said Uncle Midas, somewhat in the style of a captain giving an order — "rest there, and let us weigh what we have, lightening it with outside facts, and now and then with permissible touches of fancy. The herdsmen of Nazareth were ignorant and poor; still they complied with the Law, and at least once every year went up to Jerusalem after the custom of the feast. In the procession on one such occasion there was a family the head of which was a plain, serious-looking, middle-aged man, with whom the world has since become acquainted as Joseph. His wife, Mary, was then about twenty-seven years of age, gentle, modest, sweet-spoken, of fair complexion, with eyes of violet-blue, and hair half brown, half gold. She rode a donkey. James, Joses, Simon, and Jude, full-grown sons of Joseph, walked with their father. A child of Mary, twelve years old, walked near her. It is not at all likely that the group attracted special attention from their fellow-travellers. 'The peace of the Lord be with you!' they would say in salute, and have return in kind. More than eighteen hundred years have passed since that obscure family made that pious pilgrimage. Could they come back and make it now, the singing,

shouting, and worship that would go with them
would be without end ; not Solomon in all his
glory, nor Cæsar, nor any or all of the modern
kings, would have such attendance. Let us sin-
gle out the boy, that we may try and see him
as he was—afoot like his brethren, small, growing, and therefore slender. His attire was simple : on his head a white handkerchief, held in
place by a cord, one corner turned under at the
forehead, the other corners loose. A tunic, also
white, covered him from neck to knees, girt at
the waist. His arms and legs were bare ; on
his feet were sandals of the most primitive kind,
being soles of ox-hide attached to the ankles by
leathern straps. He carried a stick that was
much taller than himself. The old painters,
called upon to render this childish figure on canvas, would have insisted upon distinguishing it
with a nimbus at least ; some of them would
have filled the air over its head with cherubs ;
some would have had the tunic plunged into a
pot of madder ; the very courtierly amongst them
would have blocked the way of both mother and
son with monks and cardinals. The boy's face

BY THE ROADSIDE ON A ROCK

comes to me very clearly. I imagine him by the
roadside on a rock which he has climbed, the
better to see the procession winding picturesque-
ly through the broken country. His head is
raised in an effort at far sight. The light of an
intensely brilliant sun is upon his countenance,
which in general cast is oval and delicate. Under the folds of the handkerchief I see the forehead, covered by a mass of projecting sunburnt
blond hair, which the wind has taken liberties
with and tossed into tufts. The eyes are in
shade, leaving a doubt whether they are brown,
or violet like his mother's; yet they are large
and healthfully clear, and still retain the paral-
lelism of arch between brow and upper lid usu-
ally the characteristic of children and beautiful
women. The nose is of regular inward curve,
joined prettily to a short upper lip by nostrils
just full enough to give definition to transparent
shadows in the corners. The mouth is small,
and open slightly, so that through the scarlet
freshness of its lines I catch a glimpse of two
white teeth. The cheeks are ruddy and round,
and only a certain squareness of chin tells of

years this side the day the Magi laid their treasures at his feet. Putting face and figure together, and mindful of the attitude of interest in what
is passing before him, the lad, as I see him on
the rock, is handsome and attractive. When the
journey shall have ended, and his mother made
him ready for the court of the temple, he may
justify a more worshipful description; we may
then see in him the promise of the Saviour of
Men in the comeliness of budding youth, his sad
destiny yet far in the future."

Uncle Midas sank back into the ample arms
of his chair, tweaking his white mustache with
nervous fingers; and thinking to give him a rest,
Puss said: "Thank you, uncle. The figure on the
rock is ever so plain to our sight — plain as if
painted. We will wait a little if you are tired."

" I will go on," he replied. " It was only the
intrusion of that horrible Crucifixion. The plain-
er one sees the Lord the more dreadful his end
appears." The old gentleman cleared his throat
and resumed :

" 'The child grew, and waxed strong in spirit,
filled with wisdom,' is the language of the text.

Spirit, as there used, means mind, and, in the connection, *wisdom* stands for vastly more than reading and writing, more even than ability to repeat the Law and the commentaries from end to end ; it expresses all knowledge—knowledge of the high and low, of heaven and earth, of God and man; the knowledge that needs not the instruction of schools, that is not an acquisition at all, but an intuition of the universal ; a quality that cannot be better described than as an illuminated consciousness by help of which men see the truth invariably and prophesy and work miracles — in short, a quality that is itself a miracle. I do not bother asking how the lad came by the wisdom ; the words of the old Apostle are enough; they cover the process and the fact—*he filled with wisdom*. In this light the succeeding narrative becomes comprehensible ;" and raising his voice, Uncle Midas gave order, " Now read the other verses." The reader promptly responded:

"'48. And when they saw him, they were amazed: and his mother said unto him, Son, why hast thou thus dealt with us ? behold, thy father and I have sought thee sorrowing.
9

"'49. And he said unto them, How is it that ye sought me? wist ye not that I must be about my Father's business?

"'50. And they understood not the saying which he spake unto them.'"

"Ay," said Uncle Midas, with positive vehemence; "that they did not understand him helps us realize the amazing growth of the child, and how prodigiously out of the common he so early became. And then, my young friends"—his voice fell to its habitual calm assurance—"with that realization the discussion concludes itself. If any of you yet think the lad came away from Jerusalem a common boy, light-hearted, easily amused, quick at acquaintanceship, consider the effect upon him of the illuminated consciousness I have ventured in definition of what the chronicler calls wisdom. It was a light which for him reached and laid bare the infinite mysteries never so simply described as his 'Father's business.' His next appearance in Nazareth, we may well believe, was as a teacher. Up 'midst the congregation he arose, and going to the reader's place, received the sacred roll which was that Sabbath's

AT THE READER'S PLACE IN THE SYNAGOGUE

lesson. I hear the clear childish voice with which he begins, shriller growing as he advances. When at length he lifts his eyes from the page and launches into exposition, I see in their light the first suggestion of the nimbus. I see also his audience, in amazement, sunk to breathless silence ; and thinking of the Virgin Mother behind the lattice of the women's place in the synagogue, my sterner nature thrills in acknowledgment of the feeling with which she finished the white woollen gown that covered him from neck to heel, and parted his locks the night before in the style of her own, and kissed him on the full of the forehead, saying, so as to be heard by him, 'Rabbi, my rabbi—thou the Messiah ! It is good to be a handmaiden best beloved of the Lord God.' "

And as the old gentleman seemed disposed to bring his talk to an end, John ventured to speak up. " If you will pardon me," he said, " what do you understand by the term ' my Father's business ?' "

Uncle Midas gave him a serious glance, and replied :

"My dear friend, I have a faith which in the great and material things, as it is permitted me to see them, accords perfectly with the ideas of the Christian world, and it gives me an infinity of pure enjoyment. It is obvious to me that there are many things in the connection which I do not understand; these all lie out in the field of conjecture. One of the clearest observations of my life is that people of good intent are never troubled in the matter of religion except as they stray off into that field. In return for your trust in me, take a rule of conduct good for every day's observance: When you hear a man talking oracularly in definition of topics which our Lord thought best to leave outside of his teachings and revelations, set it down that he is trenching on the business of the Father and the prerogative of the Son; then go your way and let him alone. The rule is, of course, applicable only to subjects classified as religious."

Here Uncle Midas arose, and said, with his old-school politeness: "To-morrow, my young friends, or any time you choose other than to - night, I give you leave to criticise my talk upon the subject dealt with ; you may even laugh at me for having taken so many of your precious minutes in attempting to convince you that in fact Christ had no boyhood at all; but now — the fiddlers are waiting for you—"

"You are mistaken, uncle," said Nan, with twinkling eyes.

"How so?"

"They too are here, and have been for the last fifteen minutes."

"Oh! very well ; I am content with my short triumph over them. Good-night to you all."

Thereupon the company went to him one by one ; the boys shook his hand and thanked him, the girls kissed him. And the music and the dance went on till holy-day stole through the windows.

THE END.